©The Golden Dog Press, 1978

The Golden Dog Press gratefully acknowledges
the assistance accorded to its publishing
programme by the Ontario Arts Council and
The Canada Council.

ISBN # 0-919614-31-0

Printed in Canada

Introduction

Jean Baptiste, "A Poetic Olio in II Cantos, by Levi Adams" was published as a small book in Montreal in 1825.[1] The entire poem was reprinted in the February 1826 issue of *The Canadian Review and Magazine;*[2] on this occasion Adams' name was replaced by the initials "L.A." The same short form of the signature was also appended to two stories in *The Canadian Magazine* of June, 1825, and to five poems in the *Montreal Herald* between January 22, 1825 and February 22, 1826.

Very few biographical facts are available. Adams was "supposed to have been a native of the Eastern Townships" [in Lower Canada], as Henry J. Morgan reported in *Bibliotheca Canadensis* (1867). The poet's home was in Henryville, which is near the Richelieu River and Lake Champlain, not far from the American border at Rouse's Point. A French writer, Edmond Lareau, in his *Histoire de la littérature canadienne* (1874)[3] says that Levi Adam[s] "avocat", was [of] "de St. George d'Henryville,"; he does not make any clear statement about the place of Adams' birth. "L.A. Henryville, 1825," was the signature for Adams' story, "The Young Lieutenant" in *The Canadian Magazine.*[4]

Like Launcelot (the young officer of frontier militia in this tale) Adams may have passed the summer of his life "in inglorious ease," storing his mind with general and useful information, and "in particular assisting his father in the superintendence of a farm of no inconsiderable extent adjoining the family mansion." There is some support for this view in stanza X of Canto II of *Jean Baptiste.*

In 1825, or possibly earlier, Adams was a student-at-law in Montreal. According to a record in *The Montreal Almanack or Lower Canada Register for 1831,* Levi Adams' name was in the "Legal Register — Advocates, Attornies, Solicitors, Proctors, Counsel and Barristers". Adams was admitted on November 5, 1827.[5] Morgan reports the date of Adams' death: "at Montreal, of cholera, 21 July 1832." The *Montreal Gazette* gives the date as 21 June 1832.[5a]

The opening of the Little Theatre of Mr. Roy in the New Market in March 1824 afforded an opportunity for local poets to display their talents.[6] The address which was used on this occasion was chosen by a committee from poems submitted for a prize. There is no positive proof that Adams was in Montreal at the time, or that he had begun to write verse, but speculation may prove to be interesting. The winner of the New Market prize was Henry John Hagan, formerly editor of the short-lived *Literary Miscellany* (Nov. 1822-June 1823). It was Hagan's address that Adams mocked in the first stanza and the second footnote of *Jean Baptiste.* In *The Scribbler* of May 13, 1824,[7] Samuel Hull Wilcocke announced that he had "been requested to give his opinion of the two prize-addresses . . . which had been printed in Montreal papers:"

> The one which was actually spoken, written by Henry John Hagan, appeared in the *Courant;* the other, entitled *rejected address,* and which, I understand, was written by a student-at-law, is found in the Herald.

Wilcocke then paraphrased Hagan's address and commented at some length upon the one written by the student and signed X.Y.Z. The latter he said, is

> not entirely destitute of poetic merit, but is far too tame, prosaic, and didactic for theatrical recitation.

The reviewer, moreover was particularly disturbed by "the foolish and false innuendo" conveyed in the student's lines which suggested a lack of culture and education among French-Canadian youths. Wilcocke then launched a verbal attack upon the young men of the "imported part of the community, 'from beyond old ocean's tide,'." He said that they were

> generally speaking (with a few exceptions) most miserably ignorant, and contemptible objects, in a literary point of view; nor, indeed, can my powers of imagination fancy any more wretched outcast set, outcast from everything that is liberal, that is learned, that is accomplished, than the poor creatures who compose the younger part of our soi-desant [sic] British population . . . .

In comparison with Hagan's "production of a manly and independent mind," Wilcocke felt that X.Y.Z.'s *rejected address* was the work of one who had been "bred to the school of time-serving and hypocrisy,"

> He hankers after stage plays, and the vanities of the world, and in order to reconcile them with the affected puritanical sanctity of his *magnus* Apollo, whoever he is, as no doubt he has one, he concludes with the prediction
>
> Shall genius flourish, — discord no more rage, —

JEAN BAPTISTE:
A
Poetic Olio,
In II Cantos.

LEVI ADAMS

Introduction by
Carl F. Klinck

The Golden Dog Press
Ottawa — Canada
1978

And *blest religion's precepts, deck a virtuous stage?*
The harshness of Wilcocke's censure upon the work of a young student-at-law "bred in the school of time-serving and hypocrisy" may have been fired by the editor's early and almost fatal experience with the law and the courts when he was in prison charged with alleged offences against the North-West Company — and *The Scribbler* was begun in a prison cell.[8]

Adams, of course, was not the only student-at-law in Montreal, and the evidence here is not sufficient to prove that he was "X.Y.Z." But, if it was Adams who wrote the address and confused sermonizing with literary creativity, he (and his fellow-writers) would soon achieve a kind of salvation by imitating Byron's *Don Juan* (1819-1824).

Two of the lyrics by "L.A." which appeared in the *Montreal Herald* during 1825 and 1826 gave promise of nothing but outworn sentimentalism and inadequate expression: the first lines were "who has not felt hopes long delay" and "The years that I liv'd are few."[9] A third one, "Lines on a Young Lady's Glove Having Been Torn to Pieces by her Little Pug" was an effort, however ludicrous, to exploit a current fashion for burlesque:[10]

Those teeth of thine, as thou didst rend that glove,
    Wou'd I rend from thee, Pug, were I a Dentist,
But no, I may not thus my anger prove,
    For, mayhap, thou most verily repentest;
If so, I do forgive thy indiscretion,
But see, repeat not thou — the like transgression!

The *Montreal Herald* also published two instalments (November 5 and 12, 1825) of "Poetry Run Mad,"[11] a quite successful exercise in bathos, which described Montreal people in labelled groups characterized by their occupations, activities, and attitudes. "L.A.'s" special interest in the law and the courts is evident from the beginning of the first instalment:

I

Who'er has seen our Judges and our Lawyers,
    And been at Court the first day of October,
'Mongst Merchants, Grocers, Taylors, Cobblers,
    Sawyers,
    Has likewise seen full many a sad and sober
Visage and rueful countenance — alas!
That not Don Quixote's even could surpass.

II

He's seen *long robes* and *powder'd wigs* — and noses
That glisten'd like a Spanish silver dollar,
And cheeks blooming — like frost-bitten roses: —
And now and then a pale, wan-visaged scholar,
Who to his name, will sometimes write "Law
    Student."
Which chimes exactly with the word impudent.

III

He's seen, in fact, the world in miniatures
Rogue, Cheat, and Knave, Priest, Parson, Friar,
Old maids and young ones: — Dandies I am sure
Laced like a whip stick — and he 'seen the *Crier*, —
Or heard him doubtless — for his lungs are good, —
Were mine but half as strong, I would be
    understood.

IV

And he's seen men of talents — Politicians
Skill'd most profoundly, in the country's rights —
Doctors and Dentists, Charlatans, Physicians. —
He's seen — in verity — he's seen strange sights, —
And heard strange things — would that my pen were
    able,
To poetize one half the *veritable*!

V

Of learned speeches and profound orations,
Upon the "merits" of some "nice exception,"
With musty interludes of dull citations,
To prove what's clear, to the most slow perception,
Namely — that Lawyers — save to "over-reach"
Like nothing better than to make a speech!

VI

Quoth *Mr. Puff* — "hem" — "hem" — may't please
    the Court —
"Hem" — "hem" — and here I close the case,
"Fyling an affidavit to support

"What I have said." — and then, with such a grace,
Bows and sits down — when in a mighty splutter,
Up starts my "learned friend" with a "rebutter"!

In the second instalment of "Poetry Run Mad," "L.A."
described some more features of "the world in miniatures" for
which Montreal was "fam'd." Stanza VII was devoted to
journalism:
Fam'd for News-papers fill'd with *nothing new,*
Save "advertisements" and domestic trash,
A blundering *Magazine* and *"The Review",*
Where I may hope, some day, to "cut a dash,"
But the said Magazine's defunct — oh what a pity!
Were I in humour for it, I'd write its funeral ditty!

Adams may not have realized how fortunate he was to be
making his debut in Montreal when opportunities for publication
of literary pieces in that city, or indeed in the whole of Lower and
Upper Canada, had never before been so numerous and
attractive. At least three newspapers, the *Canadian Courant*, the
Herald and the *Gazette* invited literary material. There were three
notable editors, Samuel Hull Wilcocke (an emigrant from
England) and David Chisholme and Dr. A.J. Christie (both
recent emigrants from Scotland) — each one of whom
demonstrated remarkable ability in the editing of literary
journals. In St. Paul and St. François-Xavier streets there were
booksellers, publishers and printers: James Lane, Ariel Bowman,
Henry H. Cunningham, Nahum Mower, James Brown and
William Gray. Nickless and MacDonald of Notre Dame Street
not only sold books; they also operated a circulating library and
reading room.[12]

The highest literary level attempted in the 1820's in the
Canadas was in two periodicals dedicated to emulation of
Blackwood's or other imported British journals. *The Canadian
Magazine and Literary Repository* was a monthly edited by David
Chisholme from July 24, 1823 until February 1824, when he had
a dispute with the proprietor and printer, and left the magazine
which Adams described as "blundering". Dr. A.J. Christie
became editor by April 1824 and carried on until *The Canadian
Magazine* became "defunct" after June 1825. Chisholme,
meanwhile, founded *The Canadian Review and Literary and
Historical Journal* in July 1824.[13] This was the *Review* in which
Adams hoped, some day, to "cut a dash." This journal outlived
Christie's *Magazine* by one year and came to its last issue in

September 1826. What Adams did achieve in it was a complete re-printing of his *Jean Baptiste* in February 1826.

The editors of the literary periodicals favoured their own "discoveries." Wilcocke sponsored the poetical career of "Erieus" (Adam Hood Burwell), who was born in 1790 near Fort Erie in Upper Canada. Between 1821 and 1823 Burwell lived and wrote in the Talbot Settlement, farther west, on the shore of Lake Erie; at least eighteen of his poems were printed in *The Scribbler.*[14] Chisholme gave an extraordinary amount of space in his journals to the (anonymous) works of Captain George Longmore. This officer of the British Army (certainly born in Canada) has recently been identified by Mrs. Mary Lu MacDonald as a gentleman of the Staff Corps, who was the author of *The Charivari or Canadian Poetics* hidden under the pseudonym of "Launcelot Longstaff."[15] The evidence for Longmore's authorship is given in Mrs. MacDonald's introduction to a reprint of this poem by The Golden Dog Press in 1977.

Certain puzzling similarities between *The Charivari* and Adams' *Jean Baptiste* had led me, in an article in *The Dalhousie Review* of Spring 1960,[16] to propose that both poems may have been written by Adams. That guarded suggestion seemed to be secure as time went on and no challenge appeared. Now Longmore must take on what Adams must surrender. The Captain must be the author of many poems and some essays published in Chisholme's *Magazine* and his *Review* between December 1823 and February 1826. And, because some of these poems were republished in *Tales of Chivalry and Romance* (Edinburgh 1826),[17] this substantial anonymous book is also Longmore's.

Not all of the queries concerning *The Charivari* (spring 1824) and *Jean Baptiste* (1825) are swept away by the new evidence. Comparison between the two books reveals an unusual number of similarities or coincidences. Both poems reveal the current influence of Byron's *Don Juan*, especially Byron's attitudes regarding women and love, and the burlesque and bathos in his use of the *ottava rima*. As Longmore's essays reveal, he was a devoted disciple of Byron; Adams read Byron as a new master of burlesque and satire in the tradition of Samuel Butler (*Hudibras,* 1663-1678) and "Peter Pindar" (Dr. John Wolcot, author of *Lyric Odes* (1782-1785).[18]

Both poems display local colour of Montreal and the characters are French-Canadian. Longmore's Baptisto and

Adams' Baptiste are unheroic, unromantic and uncourtly figures; both are bachelors who marry at an advanced age. Baptisto's bride is a widow, Annette; Baptiste's Rosalie is a second choice after the pain of rejection by Lorrain has passed away. Both poets took pleasure in describing the weddings, the guests, and the feasts; Longmore went farther, and gave many stanzas to Baptisto's ordeal when a crowd submitted him to a charivari. Both poets revelled in observations and maxims concerning men; women; courtship; the many aspects of love; idealism and reality; marriage and its joys, bitterness and decline.

Adams goes beyond Longmore in instructing his readers, and Adams confesses to more caution about marriage than Longmore does. Love for Longmore is a glamorous, sentimental, and even classical subject; Adams' treatment of love puts it into the area of stern, practical, realities known to the legal profession and recognized in the courts.

In both books there is much realism about life in Montreal. Each author is enthusiastic about Canada — except in winter. Longmore has evidently observed with sympathy and humour the events of a French-Canadian wedding and feasting; Adams closes his poem with similar homely details about the principals and guests as Baptiste and Rosalie are united for better or for worse. Adams suggests that Rosalie is wearing a wig; Longmore displays Baptisto with, or without, his "worsted drawers and flannels." Bathos — a ludicrous and realistic descent from the elevated to the commonplace — prevails in both poems.

What conclusion is to be drawn from these two contemporary exercises in burlesque? Should they be judged as parallel imitations of *Don Juan*? Was Adams provoked or inspired to produce in 1825 an imitation of *The Charivari*? Did Adams believe that he could come closer than Longmore to the truth about human nature and French-Canadian attitudes? Was Adams, as a law-student, intent on pointing out the pitfalls of courtship and marriage which lawyers met in professional practice (see stanza LXVII, "a good marriage contract is a wise precaution.")? Or was he sardonically rationalizing his own situation as a student and a bachelor: exercised at times by doubts and by desire, feeling with Baptiste, "like one *barefooted on hot peas*!*[19]* Until critics find answers to these questions, one may rejoice that poetry of the Canadas, in its first notable awakening, provided a native setting for age-old themes — a "world in miniatures."[20]

Carl F. Klinck: The University of Western Ontario

FOOTNOTES

1. An "olio" is a medley or miscellany. The poem was "most respectfully inscribed to Stephen Sewell, Esq." — an attorney-at-law in Montreal. The first of the Latin tags, which appears in Canto I, stanza I, *"Docti indoctique scribere volunt Id est,"* both learned and unlearn'd we write,'" is attributed to "an old heathen". A similar caption stood at top of the first page of the first number of Wilcocke's *The Scribbler*. Wilcocke gave this version of the quotation from Horace: *"Scribimus docti indoctique".*

2. An alternative title for *The Canadian Review and Literary and Historical Journal*. The reference here is to Vol. II, no. IV (February 1826), 451-484.

3. (Montreal: John Lovell, 1874), p. 127.

4. *The Canadian Magazine*, IV, no. XXIV (June 1825), 495-500. Another story, "The Wedding," also signed "L.A.," *Ibid.*, pp. 523-4.

5. Thanks to Dr. Lawrence Lande, author of *Old Lamps Aglow* (Montreal, 1957) for this record.

5a. I am grateful to Mrs. Mary L. Macdonald for providing these additional biographical facts drawn from the files of the *Montreal Gazette*.

MARRIED At Northampton, Massachusetts, on Saturday the 10th instant by the Rev. Mr. Spencer, Levi Adams, Esquire of Montreal, Advocate, to Miss Elizabeth C. Wright, daughter of F.H. Wright, Equire of Northampton.
[*Gazette*, July 15, 1830]

DIED: This morning, of the prevailing malady, Levy Adams, Advocate, of this city.
[*Gazette*, June 21, 1832]

DIED: On Thursday evening, Elizabeth Wright, widow of the late Levi Adams, Esquire, Advocate, and daughter of F.H. Wright, Northampton, Massachusetts. This amiable young female survived her husband but a single day. Enfeebled by a malady from which she had scarcely recovered, she has fallen a victim to the fatigues and anxiety produced by her attendance on the sick bed of Mr. Adams whose death we announced in our last. A son, three weeks old, has been left to the care of the bereaved friends of the deceased.
[*Gazette*, June 23, 1832]

[The *Gazette* published on August 11, 1832 a Notice for settling the debts of the estate, signed by J.A. Wright, Tutor. The child evidently survived]

6. See the *Montreal Herald*, March 4, 1824.

7. V, no. 121 (May 13, 1824), 103-7.

8. See Vol. I of *The Scribbler* (Montreal, 1821-7), edited by S.H. Wilcocke.

9. *Montreal Herald*, January 22, 1825 and February 22, 1826, respectively.

10. Ibid., February 18, 1826.

11. I wish to acknowledge my indebtedness to Professor Charles R. Steele of Calgary for providing copies of these poems.

12. *An Alphabetical List of the Merchants, Traders and House-keepers Residing in Montreal* by Thomas Doidge (Montreal: John Lane, 1819).

13. The title varied: it was also known as *The Canadian Review and Magazine*.

14. *The Poems of Adam Hood Burwell* . . . Edited by Carl F. Klinck (London, Ontario: [University of] Western Ontario, *Ontario History Nuggets* No. 30, May 1963) 100 typed pages.

15. Adams' "Young Lieutenant" was also named "Launcelot".

16. XL (Spring 1960), 34-42.

17. *Op. cit.*, *"The Charivari* and Levi Adams".

18. *The Works of Peter Pindar Esq.*, with a copious Index (London: Jones and Company, 1824).

19. *Jean Baptiste*, Canto II, stanza LXII.

20. Several interesting postscripts to Adams' brief biography have been provided by courtesy of Professor Michael Gnarowski. He has found in Lareau's *Histoire* (p. 127) a reference to Adam[s], who "a laissé des poésies comiques contenues dans le *Répertoire National*, et signées *JEAN BAPTISTE.*" The *Répertoire*, edited by J. Huston, *(Montreal, 1893) Vol. I, p. 230 contains a poem, entitled "Le Beau Sexe Canadien," dated 1831 [a year before Adams' death], and signed by *"Baptiste."* This is a lyric to be sung to the air, "Charmants ruisseaux"; it is free of the complaints which characterized the *Herald* poems:
    L'air le plus pur, ces hivers sans nuages,
    Nos beaux printemps, tout ne nous dit-il pas
    Qu'un ciel ami sur nos heureuses plages,
    Sexe enchanteur, protège tes appas?
    Chantons l'amour, embellissons la vie,
    Cueillons les fleurs qu'offre notre patrie.

JEAN BAPTISTE: — *A Poetic Olio.*

MOST RESPECTFULLY INSCRIBED TO STEPHEN SEWELL, ESQR.

CANTO I.

I.

Docti indoctique scribere volunt,
  Id est, "both learned and unlearn'd we write,"*
As an old heathen said with wise intent;
  But since the Muses have been put to flight †
By scribbling scarecrows — or in dungeon pent,
  Fated to grope thro' ignorance's warning night,
'Tis deem'd in vain to stride about Parnassus
And spur the crazy Jade, yelept Pegasus.

II.

Yet some would write to keep the world in wonder;
  No matter what the subject of their theme,
Whether it be the splitting words asunder,
  Digesting sentences, — or fancy's dream,
Of bright eyes — set with lashes o'er and under,
  Of brown and black, which scarce indeed doth seem,
Worth writing verse about, tho' poets do so —
And seem as fond of trifles, as an old virtu'so)

III.

Or yet of auburn hair, in copious tresses,
  Which adds such beauty to the dimpled cheek;
Or crimson blush — that something odd expresses,
  Which truant lips would fain — but dare not speak, —
Or Ladies' 'kerchiefs, zones, or sattin dresses, —
  Item cum multis — which would take a week
To specify — in this stiff, wayward rhyme;
And at the best — 'twould be but mock sublime.

IV.

Some woo and supplicate the "tuneful nine,"
  As if they were young misses in their teens; —
Some bow submissive at their "sacred shrine,"
  And call them "Goddesses" and "heav'nly queens;"
Some choose out *one*, and her great name combine,
  With that of "mistress," whom he "humbly weens,"
Will deign to *aid* him in his bold endeavour,
To prove himself — a genius "mighty clever."

---

* Should the critical reader not like my version, he has but to give it one to suit himself.
† Vide "Prize Address" spoken at the New Market Theatre in March 1824.

V.

Another blubbers out — "aid me kind muses,
   To keep upright, astride the old jaded hack,
Of Mount Parnassus" — or perchance chooses,
   Some "gnome" or "sprite" to guide him in the track,
To fame's proud pinnacle — and thus abuses
   Their highnesses — coupling them in a pack —
Or by nick-names — at which the wise will scowl,
Pull a long face — and look much like an owl.

VI.

I'd not recriminate — tho't seems a folly —
   To sound such dreadful note of preparation;
As if the muses were abstracted — wholly
   From their employ — engaged in speculation —
Or craft of quidnune — or sate melancholly,
   Brooding, in dread, o'er future desolation; —
Or slept — and could not their assistance lend
On such obsequious vetaries to attend.

VII.

But gentle reader, let us jog along, —
   We've a good way, to journey yet together; —
And if the *muses* aid *me* in my song —
   'Tis well — if not — come rain, or windy weather —
   Should critics start and ask tho "why and whether" —
I'll stop my ears, nor heed the pedant fools,
Whilst they quote "precedent" and give their "learned rules."

VII.

Ego scribe — of matters strange and things,
   (It may be) difficult of comprehension;
Of great affairs, and mighty blusterings;
   And little wits — tho' great in self pretension,
Perhaps of courtiers, statesmen, or of kings,
   Barring to majesty all mal-intention —
Saving perchance, it might indeed seem handy,
To have some words with's Majesty a Dandy.

IX.

Which, by the bye, could scarce be deem'd high treason,
   By act of Parliament — the common law
Or learn'd precedent — nor sluggish reason,
   From whence men sometimes wise conclusions draw,
And waste the lungs and overstrain the weazon,
   To shew vast eloquence — or a small flaw!
But *Miss* or *Mister*, do not think me sinning,
For, on my word, this is but the beginning: —

X.

I mean beginning of digression, as you see,
   I've written stanzas, nearly half a score —
Just for the sake of a variety: —
   And tho' perhaps you've seen it long before,
There's a quotation — 'tis no secrecy,
   And for variety I'll quote it o'er: —
"Gutta cavet lapidum, non vi sed saepe cadendo,
"Sic homo fit doctus, non vi sed saepe scribendo."

XI.

But I — (I should have said) intend to write,
   (Not a vile critique upon this, or that,
Or desertation upon black, or white,
   Or mournful elegy on an old cat,
Nor yet the fun'ral ditty of a broken kite
   Which all well know would be confounded flat)
But what the hurthen of my tale's to be,
Have patience reader and you'll doubless see.

XII.

Yes patience — hear what I may have to say,
   It may do good, if not 'twill do no harm;
Just for amusement to pass time away —
   If, tinctured with a soporific charm,
If make you doze, — peruse it in the day —
   When you are sick, and should it grief disarm,
Tho' I am neither Doctor nor Magician —
I might set up for a most learn'd Physician:

XIII.

Perhaps give lectures — (doubtful by the way,)
   On whys and wherefores of the this, and that,
In Physic, Phthisic, Physiology — or pray?
   How would you like a lecture upon skulls, square flat
Or round heads — little difference they say —
   Except in thickness — but — but *"verbum sat"* —
Since this is but "mere moonshine,"* for oh, me!
I have, as yet, nor licence, nor diploma.

XIV.

All this for patience, which the proverb says,
   Will soothe a pain, that fretting cannot cure —
As resignation, when the good man prays,
   Marks faith unwav'ring, and a mind that's pure —

---

* And the money "Will be mere moonshine, — by and by —
tommorow."
COLEMAN'S TERENCE.

So, I cry patience; patience e'er displays
    A manly soul, that can great ills endure;
Patience will dig thro' mountains and destroy
    All opposition — patience o'ercame Troy!

XV.

Much have sage authors said, — (and say they ought)
    About great heroes — such as Paris, Nero,
Plato *et cetera* — and if I thought
    It needful, I would introduce *my* hero,
Along with ancient sages, kings "far brought,"
    Of high degree — declining down to zero,
Or modern votaries of the famed Apollo,
Whose heroes beggar all description hollow.

XVI.

In *"stricto sensu,"* as 'tis necessary,
    That I should have *one* — and to write without,
My plots and plans, would doubtless all miscarry,
    It must be that I give his name, no doubt. —
But gentle reader, if you cannot tarry,
    Till 'tis my pleasure to bring things about,
In the right way — why lay aside my verses,
Or pass a stanza — but pray spare your curses.

XVII.

Some men are heroes of their own creation,
    (A kind of satire on a good man's name,)
Who feast their pride on fond imagination,
    Or vain imaginings — 'tis much the same;
Others, to *licentia pectica,* owe derivation,
    Of their high dignity and "matchless fame:"
But my Canadian hero — JEAN BAPTISTE,
IS *"magistratus in poetica"* at least.

XVIII.

I must needs pass a few of the first years
    Of Baptiste's life — *thirty*, perhaps — or so,
The years, in which the fond idea rears,
    The fabric of its hopes — its all below,
Where these evanish — penitence and tears,
    In vain we seek — in vain indulge our woe,
Youth pass'd away — 'tis gone like life forever,
We seek her paths again — but we retrace them never!

XIX.

His youth had pass'd — the flow'r of manhood too,
    And he was bordering on that time of life,
When youthful Fancy's animated glow,

Seems lessening in fervour — and the strife
Of varying passions, in the bosom, show
The vigour of our days gone past — and rife,
With feverish anxieties, we strive to gain
Honours and wealth — with their illusive train.

XX.

I would not here pretend to undertake
  To write a satire on these Errant Knights,
Yelept *old Bachelors,* who thro' mistake,
  In their ideas of the *pure* delights,
Of being one's own self, asleep, awake,
  And at all times — renounce their *legal* rights
To social joys — the raptures and the honey,
Of the most blissful of all blisses — Matrimony!

XXI.

"Their revelries" 'tis said "are free and funny,
  "And that their days pass cheerily along —
"Mild, calm, serene, unclouded, warm and sunny —
  "As flow the numbers of some love-lorn song."
But I should deem their way was rough and stonny;
  It may be truly that I'm in the wrong: —
Tho' think of *home* — of kind and tender greeting,
Of sweet caresses, smiles — and bright eyes meeting.

XXII.

And say who'd be a Bachelor — I'd not,
  That is, if I could marry to my liking,
(Which heav'n permit may some day be my lot,)
  And get a model of each beauty striking,
In love's vocabulary — if I thought —
  But where's the rhyme? what say you now to spiking,
— Pray pardon me — I meant to add, or ought, —
That if she'd half the qualities I sought,

XXIII.

I could consent to hie me to the altar
  Of Hymen — and there for "worse for better,"
Submit to put on gentle cupid's halter,
  And lead a life — restricted to the letter,
Of matrimonial statues — nor falter,
  As did *Euripides* — whose double fetter,
Most sorely galled him, and, at length, did vex;
His very soul, with all the softer sex.

XXIV.

But Baptiste was a high life blade — that is,
  Was fond of "tissue, tinsel, gauze and shew,"

And had indeed a most expressive phiz —
  If you'd o'er seen it, you'd have thought it so —
Round as a whiskey bottle — tho' a quiz
  Was once heard say — (the *fact* I do now know,)
That Baptiste's head was large enough — but — well?
A quiz oft says what poets should not tell.

XXV.

N'importe 'tis beyond doubt he had a head,
  Fill'd with the feats of love and chivalry —
And a bold, daring heart — as it was said,
  He'd been a *voltigeur* — for liberty,
Had faced the foe — seen hosts of wounded, dead,
  And dying in life's bitter agony —
Cleft to the earth, by fate's relentless blow,
Busied in the last work of man below.

XXVI.

He'd seen all this — nay, he had seen much more,
  He'd seen two armies meet in awful fight;
Heard beating drums and the loud cannon's roar;
  Seen the day darken, as if tun'd to night,
When most terrific clouds of smoke hung o'er;
  He'd seen the foe dispersed and put to flight,
Seen what would frighten almost any hero,
His courage still abating not a zero.

XVII.

And so it chanc'd Jean Baptiste fell *"in love"*
  Poor soul, he knew not love's anxieties;
He knew not what it was his arts to prove,
  And curb the fancy, that ne'er quiet is —
Knew not how difficult it was to move
  Fond woman's heart — made up to contrarieties;
In fact (what the kind reader may discern)
Baptiste, as yet, had many things to learn!

XXVIII.

In love or *into love*, which e'er you please —
  'Tis quite the same, according as things go,
For love — 'tis said, is a most dire disease,
  And makes one feel, *"in spots, all over so!*
Though I've, as yet, not taken my degrees,
  In Cupid's College, and can't justly know:
But I will hazard *in*, for your inspection,
Saving recourse — to all who claim connection!

XXIX.

The fair *Lorrain* — some used to call her *Lady*
  (I call them all so, out of courtesy,
and yet must say, that I am often read,
  To own the epithet a falsity,)
But now, my pen, a moment pray, be steady —
  They are all pretty creatures — certes I
Ever like to treat them with docility,
For rudeness, Ladies never call civility!

XXX.

Tho' now a days, one scarce can be polite,
  Among Aunt Betty's Nieces, or bright eyes
Of mother's daughters, and e'en crack a trite
  Old joke, thro' which, prechance there might arise,
A little tittering — but "all's not right" —
  And *Miss* is quaintly told — "If she is wise,
"To be upon her look out" — not to mention
The Cunning hint of "dubious intention:"

XXXI.

With a long sermon on "female propriety,"
  Thus ringing thro' the town a false alarm;
And altho' now and then I love variety,
  And think that mixing with the world's no harm —
To study out the mysteries of society; —
  I must allow, to me, there is no charm,
In seeing every day new fashions, or *Ma's pet*,
Push'd in the face of common sense — a starch'd coquette!

XXXII.

The fair Lorrain, whose name perforce I give —
  And 'tis a pretty name — and so was she;
I'll not describe her — tho' I do believe,
  Perhaps a prettier, fairer, ne'er could be;
Some say there have been — but they must forgive
  My deeming them mistaken: Old Hebe,
Whom poets tell of, nor yet Grecian Helen,
Who with the vagrant Paris so deep fell in

XXXIII.

Love — were never half so lovely I opine.
  But I'm no limner — ergo — cant paint faces
In common colours, much less in divine,
  With the minutia of eyes, lips, grimaces,
And the "and so forth," which we need combine,
  With a fair form, to model for the graces.
She was of that description — on my life —
I'd choose her counterpart — were I to choose a wife.

XXXIV.

She lived in Canada — no matter where,
    It might be cloistered in a nunnery,
Breathing a life of solitude and prayer,
    In sweet seclusion from all reveiry.
Or it might be, that she did choose to share
    The smiles of an ungrateful world, and see
The fickleness of man — inconstancy and folly,
Now smiling, angry, gay or melancholly.

XXXV.

"False colours last" — like tints on beauty's cheek,
    An hour they sparkle like the diamond bright;
Then fade — their lovely shade in vain we seek,
    Dimm'd by time's cruel, unrelenting blight.
"False friends will smile," an hour, a day, a week,
    Then friendship, with ingratitude requite —
And wound the breast that hath too dearly learned,
No pang, is like the pang, of kindness — ill returned!

XXXVI

I had a "friend" once, and I deem'd him all,
    That man could or should be — not what man is,
And has been, e'er since our first parents' fall
    From Eden's bow'rs — blest Paradise of bliss —
But he is changed; what *then* was friendships' call
    Were now a favour to bestow — but 'tis
Not, not that I grieve, the moments past to scan;
I grieve to see th' inconstancy of man.

XXXVII.

I said no matter where she lived — 'tis true —
    The where and how do not much signify;
She lived — good reader that's enough for you —
    So pray discard your curiosity:
Since to that secret should you get "the clue,"
    You'd think yourself to be, as wise as I! —
And in an author's whole vocabulary,
No word, than — "self-importance" is more necessary!

XXXVIII.

What say you reader? — Didst e'er read "Broad grins?"
    (It is bound up with "my night gown and slippers.")
If you have not, go read it for your sins,
    And tell me, if, you've e'er, among verse clippers,
Found one could clip more quaintly "Outs and Ins,"
    And sometimes *nip* close as a pair of nippers.
But reader, if your patience, I've borne hard on,
I must beg leave to beg your patience's pardon.

XXXIX.

I then proceed. From some unknown reason,
   (Love never asks for ' reason, nor for rhyme.")
Baptiste now felt — what will forever tease one,
   When either out of season, place, or time.
It was now what is called "domestic treason,"
   But a strange feeling rather more sublime:
Inflammatory in its variations,
Symptoms: — pulse quick, cheeks hectic, and heart palpations!

XL.

He felt, "somehow" a kind of anxious spell,
   And sometimes most sententiously would sigh.
The Ladies did conjecture him *unwell*,
   Mal-à-la-tête — and hoped he would not die!
King hearted Ladies! I the truth must tell,
   I love you, as I love my own right eye:
Kind and yet cruel, and pray where's the wonder,
You smile awhile, then rend mens' hearts asunder.

XLI

In truth the world's a wonder altogether —
   And man's a creature wonderfully made, —
(And so is woman!) fickle as the feather;
   So heathenish philosophers have said,
Made to endure sunshine and rainy weather,
   To love, fear, hope, betray and be betrayed,
And marry too — not till he courts a wife tho',
Eat, drink, be merry, some say smoke tobacco.

XLII.

That is, as one methinks should comprehend it,
   To feel quite pleased when things go "smooth and clever:"
And when a little rough, to condescend t'it,
   Because to tease, and I fret and scold will never,
Lessen an ill, when one cannot forefend it. —
   To love when inclination prompts, if ever
An object worthy of our love be found; —
To fear; — when any thing the sense confound.

XLIII.

Get married, aye — but more of this ere long —
   To eat when one is hungry — drink when dry,
Be merry when in humour for a song,
   That is, when melancholly is not nigh,
Peace reigns within, and nothing seemeth wrong:
   In other words, when one feels "very high,"
Can give and take a joke, and chase hence sorrow,
and keep his conscience harmless for the morrow.

XLIV.

And as for smoking, just as one would please,
  Joking, I'd relish better, but "you know,"
Not every one can take things at their ease,
  And some are vapid as the chilling snow,
Cold, murky, saturnine, — and endless tease
  One with their nonsense, — dogged, dull and slow, —
I hate it all, and think that a good *smoker*,
Should smoke away, and never set up joker.

XLV

Jean Baptiste lov'd his pipe as well as any
  Man, of like sensibility, could do —
Tho' not so inordinately as many,
  Who whiff, and puff, and smoke, the whole week thro'!
Yet when the weather was or dull, or rainy,
  He could, at leisure, smoke a pipe or so:
Which serves (*I'm told*) to help one's cogitations,
And brighten up dull paced — imaginations!

XLVI.

He lov'd a joke — in common acceptation,
  When aimed either 'gainst a foe or friend:
And could laugh heartily in approbation,
  When not obliged his batteries to defend, -
And perchance give a shout for prolongation;
  When the result no danger did portend;
But for all this — tho' Baptiste was "no fool,"
Much did he dread the shafts of ridicule!

XLVII.

And for myself, I think they truly are,
  What it requires some patience to endure;
So exquisite the pain, we're forced to bear,
  Against our will; (which grieves us doubly sore;)
And like the rheumatism, that with great care,
  And scores of nostrums we can seldom cure;
But there's one consolation, if they wound: —
"A dart well parried, may perchance rebound,"

XLVIII.

If with her shafts — Baptiste was e'er afflicted,
  He would send forth a "genteel oath or two,"
As anger sate upon his brow depicted,
  And deemed them handy as small clothes, altho'
He ne'er stark mad profainity affected,
  More than such men of quality perforce do,
Merely to shew an "independant spirit,"
Or man with "wonderful degree of merit."

XLIX.

Now Baptiste was indeed a "man of state,"
   Not that he kept a dashy coach and six,
While throngs of minions on his nod await,
   But was (not to be tedious or prolix)
A famous politician; and could prate
   About the *"Civil list,"* and rightly fix,
In his own mind, when to relax and give —
And how to "exercise prerogative."

L.

"Religion et Liberté" did much disturb
   His ineditations, for much did he fear,
The civil power should dare attempt to curb,
   Or stint him, in the use of blessings, e'er
So just and highly praised, — and our superb
   Constitution, which he held so dear,
Might most unluckily be taken from us —
When we might put on sackcloth, or invoke St. Thomas!

LI.

But my good reader, let us *veer* about. —
   I hate all politics upon my word;
And politicians too, they make such rout
   For a mere trifle; tho' Byron, you have heard,
Or I will tell you, could not do without
   Them — (such good wholesome lessons they afford,)
And brought them in, for sake of their variety,
"To stuff with *sage* that verdant *goose* society."

LII.

Tho' not professedly a moralizer —
   One may presume to lecture, now and then,
E'en those who are, in truth, much wiser
   Than his dear self; since there's a class of men,
Who sadly need, a candid, kind adviser,
   And, might derive instructions, from my pen; —
But stop — my pen is bad — and I must mend it —
So ends the stanza — or this line will end it!

LIII.

"A love scene and good dinner are fine things"
   Among the joys and disappointments of this life —
And yield "true bliss" — as nature's minstrel sings —
   If true bliss there may be, where all is rife
With vexation, ambition, riotings,
   Distrust deceit, contention, woe and strife;
I hate the former — though as I'm a sinner;
I dearly love a savoury, wholesome dinner.

22

LIV.

And who that does not? but these sad "love scenes,"
    Awaken recollections in the mind,
Of woeful hours; like grief that intervenes
    To mar our dearest blessings, or some kind
Star, that with gracious influence, half leans,
    In palid splendour, and seems not unkind,
But yields no consolation from that sorrow,
Which waits to canker each returning morrow.

LV.

   * * * * * * * * *
    * * * * * * * *

Who has not felt that wasting, pensive feeling,
    That springs from young affections sadly crossed,
Over the recollections hourly stealing,
    Like the remembrance of some dear friend lost,
He who hath, knows sorrow — he who hath not,
Has yet, to learn what "cannot be forgot."

LVI.

I said that Baptiste loved — and loved full well,
    Tho' not with that soft sensibility, —
Which binds the young heart in Elysian spell,
    Or robs it of its calm tranquility,
And of a fairy Eden seems to tell,
    Where all is mildness, kindness and docility.
His love, in sooth, was wonderfully curious,
Neither too cold, nor absolutely furious.

LVII.

'Twas a strange mixture of that vanity,
    Incident to a light fantastic mind, —
Ne'er sensible of its own inanity —
    And natal weakness, and that mongrel kind,
Of feeling, bord'ring on insanity;
    And which leaves its feeble votary blind,
To nature's impulse. — a nameless love or a,
(If courteous critics will allow,) *"lusus natura."*

LVIII.

He lov'd — but sadly was his love returned. —
    Lorrain ne'er cheer'd him with those "anxious smiles,"
Which speak the heart — and in her bosom burn'd,
    No tender passion, that this life beguiles
Of half it woes — but cruelly she spurn'd,
    Or seem'd to spurn, his most assiduous wiles
To please, which griev'd full sore his wounded heart,
And vexed him, with intolerable smart.

LIX.

I love to eulogize the sex sincerely —
  Their sweetness, kindness, gentleness of soul;
'Tis said they're fickle, — yet I love them dearly: —
  I love to dwell on that fond spell which stole;
My young affections; and had nearly,
  Bereft me of my own weak heart's controul;
The warmth of feeling growing to excess, —
In blissful transports words cannot express!

LX.

O yes, — there are in youth, those happy hours,
  Those trembling moments of supreme delight,
We would not barter for, nor thrones, nor powers,
  Nor all that e'er could mock the wand'ring sight,
Or strike the fancy — could we call them ours,
  And safe preserve them, from the cruel blight,
Of rolling years, which marrs our dearest joys, —
Our fondest hopes — and happiness destroys.

LXI.

But I will check my Pegasus — and draw —
  My half-prose-olio to a conclusion.
Perhaps 'tis faulty — I dont care a straw —
  Who, or what is not? tho' I hate confusion,
And like things uniform, and without flaw —
  Or that abound in beauty to profusion,
But who would choose become an analytic,
Merely to please a despicable critic?

LXII.

I said Lorrain ne'er felt the sweet delight,
  Arising from a passion in the breast,
Called Love — soft agonizing bliss — the bright,
  Delirious vision of pure rest —
And holy raptures — but I love to write
  The truth, — Baptiste had ne'er her love possessed; —
She loved, (all women do,) and at length married,
When Baptiste found his hopes had all miscarried.

LXIII.

I know not how it is — but there are those,
  Who can, but sadly, these sad ills endure,
In love affairs — who look moody, morose,
  Impatient, melancholly and demure,
As if no tongue could tell out half their woes,
  And no physician their disorder cure;
Or, as if, grief was fetter'd to a mind,
That could not bear one ill of life resigned.

LXIV.

And there are those who pass regardless over,
  Such disappointments, and with care deface,
Each fond remembrance, of a cruel lover,
  That, in mind, had long held welcome place;
Others, some small disquietude, discover,
  But strive to bear them with a seeming grace,
And an assumed fortitude display,
As if ashamed their weakness to betray.

LXV.

Poor Jean Baptiste had no such fortitude,
  No kind resource of soothing consolation,
Arising from within — that might elude
  The wasting pang of silent desolation,
That prey'd upon a mind, by love beshrew'd;
  Nor soothing hope t'extend alleviation, —
Or cheer him with her palliating rays —
And shed bright prospects on his future days.

LXVI.

I cannot say he was *"non compos mentis"*
But on his brow sat such a woeful look
  Of angry sorrow, that ne'er content is,
You would have thought kind reason had forsook
Her post, — and, as when life's weak thread, half spent is,
  And seems too slender nature's throe to brook.
Awful he pin'd in melancholly sorrow —
And seem'd life's every mental grief to borrow.

LXVII.

But soon his anguish grew to desperation,
  And death only promis'd a quick release,
From pain and sorrow's dreadful devastation: —
  "The soul must be disbanded" — Death was peace" —
Next came the blasphemous determination —
  The fatal, dire, resolve — but does life cease?
No Sirs — hanging infused such a queer pain,
It brought him to his senses back again.

LXVIII.

'Twas that or else the fall — for in a blunder
  He'd ta'en a 'kerchief for the fatal deed, —
Which broke, like Sampson's flaxen cords asunder,
  And kindly eased him down"
          * * * * * * * *
        * * * * * * *
Much did he grieve, that it had not been stronger,
But, thought it best, — *to live a little longer!*

LXIX.

I'm glad he thought so — glad indeed, —
    For if he had not — mournful to relate
Here must have closed my story with the deed,
    Which would have sealed poor Baptiste's wretched fate,
And put a *"Finis* to the *Tome*: — so speed
    Thee yet, my Pegasus, — write — rhyme — but wait —
I promis'd a respite — or short reprieve —
The weaknesss of the Ladies' weak eyes to relieve!

LXX.

And so farewell! the kindest friends must part,
    And absent feel the silent loneliness, —
The gloomy chasm of an aching heart,
    That spurns the proffer of a cold caress!
Awhile farewell! — at this, the tear may start,
    And flow — but it hath less of bitterness, —
Less of the pang, we feel, when fortunes sever
Two fond adoring hearts — in life — forever!
(End of the first Canto.)

JEAN BAPTISTE: — *A Poetic olio.*

CANTO II.

I.

Oh! Canada — fair land of freedom styled —
  Land of the meadow, mountain, hill and dale;
Of winter stern — spring calm, and summer mild,
  Of sweeping tempest, of soft murm'ring gale,
I love thy prospects — thy lone forests wild, —
  Thy changes, from when winter's blasts assail, —
To the warm breeze of spring — from loneliness
A field, to summer's fairest, greenest dress.

II.

I love thy boundless wastes — thy solitudes,
  Where savage man, from savage man may stray,
And seek, unaw'd — (scarce other care intrudes,)
  The seanty pittance of each coming day;
Without a hope, that present peace deludes,
  Of fame or greatness — in his lonely way —
Content to live — a pilgrim's life to roam;
Fixed to no spot — at home — without a home.

III.

I love thy cataracts and flowing tides —
  Thy wild romantic falls — I love — alas!
No more — what woe that fatal word betides —
  I lov'd once tenderly — but let it pass —
I would forget that time — yet still it glides
  Across my memory — as life's low glass,
Seems running out — remembrance cannot die —
Slow — cankering gangrene of all misery!

IV.

"Care to our coffin adds a nail" says Brome,
  Or Pindar, or some other versifier, —
Whether bedoom'd earth's dirty face to roam,
  To satiate an ambitious bold desire;
Or cooped up, in our little "house and home,"
  Like a poor felon, parson, nun, or friar, —
And that a "jovial, merry song" (no doubt
(Sung o'er a can of ale) "will draw it out."

V.

But "love adds two" — for reader think the number,
  Of melancholly visages you meet,
Heedless of earthly din — as lifeless lumber —
  Whene'er you pass along a well lin'd street,
In our good City: — think of those who slumber —
  Beneath the clod, whereon men tread their feet;
Cut down in life's young prime, and the presumption,
That half, perhaps, or more died with a love consumption.

VI.

Aye, think of this: — and if you have a heart,
  (Or young or old) I pray you guard it well,
From the assault of bright eyes, — and the dart
  Of wonder working — Cupid, cruel, fell,
Barbed and keen pointed, to inflict a smart
  Which, 'twere in vain here to attempt to tell,
The anguish — but this much I can assure ye,
That many thousand songs will never cure ye,

VII.

Or draw the nail out — I suppose you'd have it,
  By the way of keeping up the metaphor.
What is a metaphor? — But *gutta cavet"* —
  I stated somewhere back — why, or what for,
Or what — need not be told — tho' if you crave it,
  Vide Canto first, verse tenth. Oh, I abhor
These niceties — how much so — and how ample —
I think my proem a most excellent ensample.

VIII.

— I love to wander, at the set of sun,
  The fair St. Lawrence's downing stream beside,
Now watch her smoothly limpid waters run,
  Then list the gurgling, rippling, rolling tide,
Or view the proud ship — her long voyage done —
  Safe into port, with look majestic ride,
And furl her unfurl'd sails — her anchor cast,
Heedless of future, or of dangers past.

IX.

I love to contemplate the dawning night,
  When darkness sinks by slow degrees around;
Just so age steals upon the mental sight,
  And leaves the intellect in sorrow bound!
I love to watch pale Luna's trembling light,
  When first she breaks upon night's deep profound:
Her rays are brilliant, but evanish soon,
And tell all changeable and fickle as the moon.

X.

Ah! then my thoughts turn back to other days,
　　To home — sweet spot, and fondly cherish'd too —
To youthful scenes — where fancy still portrays,
　　The garden, grot, the elm, the shady yew,
The babbling brook that winds along the maze,
　　Of shrubbery and thorn — the distant view
Of spreading tields; — the lambkins sporting there;
My FATHER's kindness and my MOTHER's care!

XI.

Youths glowing hours are sunny hours — in vain,
　　We pause, to count them and recount them o'er,
To watch their fleetness — passing in the wane!
　　As the lone mariner looks on the shore,
We look with trembling vision, — gaze again, —
　　We sleep — we dream, and wake, they are no more —
No more delude our fancy — hopeless gone —
　　Youth's glowing hours, we call but once our own.

XII.

Go look upon the smiling infant — see
　　What thou hast been — how beautiful — how fair —
Its rosy cheek — it turns and smiles, on thee:
　　Then look upon thy aged parent's — where
Thou may'st read, what thou ere long, *shalt* be;
　　For there are wrinkles, and deep furrows there, —
And lines betokening grief, and days of woe,
And locks about them like the hoary snow!

XIII.

Go to the silent tomb — and cast thine eye
　　Around — and look upon the cold, damp earth;
Together infants and the aged lie,
　　In quiet, 'neath the grassy turf — no mirth,
Or riot, heedless laugh, or revelry,
　　Shall there mock thy meditations; — a dearth
Of all — but silence and sad thoughts — thoul't find;
Youth's sunny hours shall break not on thy mind!

XIV.

They think not of thy youthful hours — the years
　　Of bye-past-scenes 'tis bitterness of thought;
Nay dream not of them — they were full of tears
　　Of restlessness — and "hopes delay'd" — and fraught
With griefs, thy memory tells not of, — and fears
　　Of coming woes — but look beyond, where taught
To soar, faith triumphs o'er death's dark, cold bed,
And, all immortal, man no tears shall shed.

XV.

"Yet there are thoughts that cannot die;" — the blast
    Of keen adversity may keenly sweep,
And blight our young hopes — and the long, the last
    Ling'ring ray, that seem'd awhile to keep,
Its throne within our bosoms, may go past, —
    The impress still remains — engraven deep
Upon the heart, — still thoughts, there are, that press
Around that "throne of silent loneliness."

XVI.

```
*  *  *  *  *  *  *  *  *
  *  *  *  *  *  *  *  *
*  *  *  *  *  *  *  *  *
  *  *  *  *  *  *  *  *
*  *  *  *  *  *  *  *  *
  *  *  *  *  *  *  *  *
*  *  *  *  *  *  *  *  *
  *  *  *  *  *  *  *  *
```

XVII.

Call you it madness to write poetry?
    I grant it may be madness to excess, —
But who loves not soft soothing minstrelsy,
    Awakening feelings tongue cannot express; —
Who does not feel transporting ecstacy —
    With dear delusion the whole soul possess —
List'ning the poet's sweetly flowing numbers,
Sacred and pure as "evening's silent slumbers?"

XVIII.

Who does not love the music of the grove,
    When warbling songsters chaunt their notes at eve,
Making sad moan, or telling tales of love,
    While rustling grove, in gentle murmurs heave,
And thro' the glade, the sighing breezes move,
    And to the throng their little echoes give?
Or sit and gaze on amoret's glowing eyes,
As, from her tongue, sweet notes of concord rise?

XIX.

'Tis he alone whose bosom never glows,
    With soft sensations and ethereal joys;
Who hath no tear to sooth a fellow's woes,
    When inward peace corroding grief destroys; —
He who ne'er tastes that sacred sweet repose,
    The calm, compassionative soul enjoys —
But morbid, insensate, unfeeling, slow, —
Content alike life's joys and sorrows to forego.

XX.

But music, poetry, or politicians,
　　With all their maxims, measures, tones and feet,
'Tis much the same; we call those wise physicians,
　　Who keep the constitution in complete
State of preservation; and those magicians,
　　Bards or minstrels (choose which you will *ensuite*,
As I'm in haste) who with their minstrelsie,
Makes us forget, what sort of folk we be.

XXI.

"There's music in all things, if men had ears" —
　　Says Byron, that is; if men had ears to hear,
For if they had not, plainly it appears,
　　The sweetest note that e'er drew forth a tear,
From maiden fair, as mirth's obstreperous cheers,
　　Or winds that bleakly sweep the forest drear,
Pass o'er the deadly corse, would pass him by,
Or march of death at midnight — silently!

XXII.

But while on music, tones and variations,
　　Let's vary still — as we're not stational; —
To other subjects turn our lucubrations,
　　Keeping within the sober bounds of *rational*;
And tho', indeed, I like not alterations,
　　On matters private, learned or national,
Yet, just to see, what one perforce can do,
I shall attempt, to write a verse or two,

XXIII.

Upon nicknames. And first there's *Jonathan*,
　　A fellow, cunning and "curious" as "tarnation;" —
Is seldom certain — but to guess, swear, van,
　　And hit the mark, in *"spec."* or "calculation!"
Which he will do as well as any can,
　　Considering his *"home-made* education!"
Altho' 'tis thought, by those who ape their betters,
He'll soon become a *"real man of letters!"*

XXIV.

I'd like to see the matter realized,
　　And, ere while, prove in truth a staunch reality: —
For if, he lov'd the being catechised,
　　One half as dearly as he loves *equality*,
In a few years, I would not be surpris'd,
　　To find him all *refinement"* and *"formality,"*
And not to imitate his neighbours, speak,
Some learn'd lingo — as Hebrew, Latin, Greek!

XXV.

There's stubborn, stiffneck'd, old *"John Bull,"*
　Who boasts that a monstrous deal of common sense:
It must be blunt, if suited to the skull,
　(Which seems of course th' attendant consequence,)
Thick, dogged, and impenetrably dull,
　That proves a bulwark in its own defence:
But, true it is, he is a blustering fellow,
And like most others — knows well when to "bellow."

XXVI.

There's *Paddy* — a strange compound of oddities,
　And contrarieties of Bulls and *blunders*,
With "och! my honey," — "faith!" and such commodities,
　As wit from reason fancifully sunders —
But Pat's is a good soul — "odds 'sblood it is," —
　He loves the Ladies — arrah! and who wonders,
I love them too — *Pat* is a Lady's man —
I would be there too, — who would not pray, that can?

XXVII.

There's honest *Sawney* "ganging bock again" —
　Honest indeed, as honesty now passes —
He keeps one eye to't — th'other to his gain)
　Or rather half of one — in common cases, —
Unless its sore, and gives him too much pain: —
　But Sawney has the soncy bonny lasses,
With rosy cheeks — and they are not so stupid.
As 'nae to ken the wily arts o' Cupid."

XVIII.

Thus much: Now for the hero of my story —
　Poor *Baptiste's* love, which had been so long crescent,
Began to wane — he'd reach'd the *"heighth of glory,"*
　And see her splendours passing, evanescent;
But luckily escaped the promontory
　Of ruin — soon growing convalescent; —
So, by the time a few months had passed over,
He look'd as cheerful — as a field of clover.

XXIX.

'Tis true, he had his mournful recollections,
　And bitter visions, that forever tease one.
Oft would he sigh out broken interjections,
　And press his bosom, as if just to ease one
Swelling thought, that recall'd crossed affections,
　And seldom listen'd, or to "rhyme, or reason:"
Regretting much the want of fortitude,
To bear with patience, or with skill t'elude.

XXX.

Oh, Love! to write it makes my heart ache sadly;
    In truth, I love to have it ache a little, —
Not that I'd feel the tender passion madly,
    But to remind me that life's thread is brittle,
And quickly may be snapp'd — I would not, gladly,
    Feel as poor Baptiste did, in every tittle,
Nor in the outline, but there are sensations —
Most deeply painful with *their* consolations.

XXXI.

Oh love! or Cupid, with thy well lin'd quiver,
    Author of half the misery of this world;
How oft, the young, romantic mind, to shiver,
    Hast thou thy little darts of ruin hurl'd,
Infusing poison to the poet's liver, —
    Or keenly pointed, at a venture whirled,
Thy wrathful *Plenipos,* in vengeful rage,
Like the proud warrior of Egyptian age.

XXXII.

Oh, love — mysterious, heterogeneous, feeling,
    Pleasant enough, when no sharp pang of sorrow,
In painful, gloomy, retrospection stealing
    Upon the mind, — beclouding each to morrow, —
And in a mass of torpid grief congealing
    The passions, that from faithless hope, would borrow,
Some antidote, to check the perturbation,
Which thrills the soul with silent desolation.

XXXIII.

Oh Love! minstrel of shady groves and bowers,
    Of mountain valley, wood — of every where;
Sweet harbinger of bliss of bridal flowers,
    Connubial rapture, and connubial care; —
Of glowing visions, — of kind soothing hours, —
    And dark foreboder of forlorn deapair!
I would not love — (reason and prudence bid not)
Could I endure life's burthen if I did not.

XXXIV.

So Baptiste thought, at least so 'twould appear, —
    He loved full dearly, but his love was slighted,
And hopes long cherished with distrust and fear,
    Were cruelly and mercilessly blighted, —
He ponder'd oft — and oft let fall a tear,
    And seem as if his spirits were benighted, —
Till time and chance, true friends to the ill-fated —
His love-impressions quite — *obliterated*!

XXXV.

So changeable — so wavering is man;
   Full of inconsistency and fickleness;
Chequered with hopes and fears — his narrow span
   Soon wastes away; — now fondness to excess —
Now coldness to reserve. Indeed, to scan
   His way, were hard, so given to transgress
All rules: tho' all, 'tis said, with a firm resolution,
May be achiev'd by time and a good — constitution!

XXXVI.

I can't say whether 'twas a year, or more,
   After Baptiste so 'gregiously had erred;
At all events, some few months had passed o'er
   Or by and under (which is most preferred,
By learn'd *gents*) it might have been a score,
   Or less — when to our hero it occur'd:
That tho' he'd eaten many a wholesome fish —
"As *good remaine'd* — as e'er yet *grac'd a dish*!"

XXXVII.

Apropos of fishing — alias angling —
   Altho' to fish in "muddy waters" much,
I ne'er could bear — 'tis so like household wrangling —
   (A subject which I ever hate to touch
Upon — it savoureth so much of strangling;)
   I really could not object to such
A thing as fishing — in a limpid fountain, —
Deep, clear and bright, — beside some lofty mountain: —

XXXVIII.

Not in a wood — for all this world's bothers,
   I never knew a greater botheration, —
(With just one *salvo* — which I keep from others,
   Through mere principles.) — that the sole vexation
Of being bitten by musquetoes: — who smothers
   Then his *ire* — if I'm good in calculation,
Would make a second *Job*, and in the *ashes*,
Sit down quite patiently, and cut himself in — gashes!

XXXIX.

But in the open field — with here and there,
   A shady elm, or lowly willow bending —
In pensive stillness — heedless of all care,
   Or ruthless danger, ruthlessly impending,
I'd wander — while old Sol shone bright and fair,
   His warm beams to the cold earth lending; —
And it is said — the truth I do not doubt,
One need not fish long now-a-days, — *"to catch a trout."*

XL.

— In truth, tho' Baptiste could not love another,
  Or said as much, it proved quite *au contraire.*
So fate would have it, — and not all the pother
  Of his reason, (which was indeed *très clair,*)
Could a young bud of *"infant"* passion smother;
  Attempted with the most assiduous care: —
I would not say — his love was predestined, —
Nor thing of chance — for no true end designed.

XLI.

"I hold the world, but as the world" — a thing
  "Of shreds and patches," botched up and mended,
Like an old worn out coat, with scarce a string
  Of the original; — and man descended, —
Retaining in descent, but "griefing and sorrowing,"
  From the first parent: — together blended,
The world and its frail tenant, — and highly rated,
Would prove, I think, most woefully degenerated.

XLII.

Things after cases — cases circumstances —
  And circumstances, when combined together,
Affect strange wonders in our fickle fancies.
  Even that insubstantial thing a feather,
Like the proud ship that on the rough surge dances,
  Mocking the heavy anchor's feeble tether,
Instructs the mind,* on sober contemplation,
And feasts, perchance for hours our meditation.

XLIII.

Thus man's life passes — and the contrariety,
  Of woes, vicissitudes, pain and distress,
He here doth undergo, in sad variety, —
  For him to own it full of bitterness. —
  * * * * * * * * *
    * * * * * * * *
  * * * * * * * * *
    * * * * * * * *

XLIV.

There's bitterness in youth — tho' strew'd with flow'rs,
  It is a wayward, thorny, crooked course, —
Now we recline in soft Elysian bowers,

---

* CHAUCER. speaking of the inspirer of his numbers, says: —
  "Her divine skill taught me this;
  "That from every thing I saw,
  "I could some instruction draw."

And drink pure pleasure from its purest source;
Now we are sad — and disappointment lowers,
And sinks the soul with an o'erwhelming force.
With all youth's feverency and ardour bright,
We love— and cherish hopes to feel their blight.

XLV.

A heart too tender and that feels too much,
    Experience, reason tell is bitterness —
'Tis bitterness, when fancy's glowing touch,
    Paints pining sorrow in her sadest dress,
To feel, — (alas why is our nature such,)
    We cannot ease the object in distress.
'Tis bitterness to see bedew'd with tears,
A father's cheek — grown pale with grief and years!

XLVI.

There's bitterness in love we cant endure,
    To know that we have lov'd and lov'd in vain,
To seek the little bark — (in hope made sure,)
    That did our dearest, fondest hopes contain,
And floated on the tide of life secure,
    For months, — perhaps for years, — bewreck'd amain,
On disappointment's ruthless shoals — and see
How near allied are love and — misery.

XLVII.

There's bitterness in silent dark suspense,
    While hope still lingers, and yet scarcely beams,
And the soul wanders tremblingly intense,
    And seeks her object in lone midnight dreams,
Or fleeting visions, that deceive the sense,
    And mock our sighs with hope's delusive gleams!
There's bitterness in song — and if I'm right in guessing —
The reader findeth bitterness in my — digressing.

XLVIII.

The lady *Rosalie* was one of those
    Belles Dames, tutor'd to think, (I know not why)
That married life yielded — no such repose, —
    As might be found in sweet celibacy.
"Experiencia docet" — the maxim goes, —
    Which she had had to a staunch certainty:
As she'd nigh reach'd her puberty I ween,
That is — some eight and twenty winters seen.

XLIX.

She bore the stmp, by some esteemed pretty, —
    Nearly five feet, — but was not over slender;

Her face was comely, her eyes somewhat jetty,
  Looked languishing, impassionate and tender,
And e'en could ogle; — (and pray where's the pity?)
  In fine, she was so form'd — one would commend her
Tout ensemble, rather than criticize, —
Tho' not perhaps, what all would idolize.

L.

At Church, (she was a *Catholic* good reader,)
  With holy ardour, she devotion paid;
And at the altar seem'd a constant pleader,
  Her life, with innocence might be pourtray'd:
I cannot say but, that sometimes indeed, her
  Gentle soul from church devotion strayed;
But when she raised her eyes — so haven beguiling, —
You'd almost thought you saw an — angel smiling.

LI.

Matins and *Vespers* rigidly she kept,
  With holy *Lent*, fasting and *abstinence*,
And o'er her *pater nosters* oft she wept
  "So modestly *faisant la pénitence*.". . . .
        * * * * * * * * *
          * * * * * * * *
        * * * * * * * * *
          * * * * * * * *

LII.

I said she pin'd in single blessedness,
  Merely because her Ladyship so chose
To do, — and had her notions to excess;
  I could not say exact how many beaux,
There had been, who attachment did possess; —
  Or if she'd any — though one would suppose,
By the account that at least eight or nine,
Had bow'd obsequious at her beauty's shrine.

LIII.

But let that pass — as they had pass'd away —
  She'd reach'd the years of prudence and discretion,
And felt that every hour and every day,
  Left her one less — *to live* — and the impression,
That all her youthful beaux and sweethearts gay
  Had fled, would often force the sad confession,
(To private friends) that should she meet an offer, —
Blest be the hand — that first good luck might proffer.

LIV.

I know not how — but like all other stories,
  Of like importance — 'twas soon circulated,
From this to that — (like cant of whigs and tories,)
  And came to Baptiste's ears, who quite elated,
Appear'd as if he'd yield the ghost before his
  Time was come; and, with impatience, waited
The happy moment, when he might disclose,
Something that in his anxious breast arose.

LV.

Think you 'twas Love?* It might be nicknamed such,
  But on my word I would not call it so.
Perhaps 'twas the reason, those oft boast so much,
  Who yet can scarce "old Bachelor" forego, —
And seek a wife — with a prometheau touch,
  Of itching passion — near akin to snow; —
It might have been dear bought philosophy, —
But what it was it does not signify.

LVI.

Next holiday to church with great devotion —
  He went — with look demure, downcast and lowly;
And in his breast there seem'd a warm emotion,
  As loud he sang in chorus sad and slowly:
And then the *Messe* did raise such sweet commotion,
  Of heavenly ardour and of fervour holy,
You would have thought (think otherwise you can)
He was, in the reality, a godly man.

LVII.

Fair Rosalie beheld him with delight,
  Joining *en messe*, with such a modest grace;
Indeed, she felt enraptured at the sight,

---

* As it is a pretty generally received custom among men of literary habits, never to lose a good opportunity of displaying the extent and profundity of their reading, — though of very modest and humble pretentions and one who would by no means wish to be thought "wise over much," I cannot prevail upon myself, on the present occasion, to omit giving the following quotation from Butler's Hudibras; — partly for the aforesaid reason, but more particularly for the information of the Ladies, whose respectful votary I hold myself at all times to be:
  "Though Love be all the world's pretence,
  "Money's the mythologic sense,
  The real substance of the shadow,
"Which all address and courtship's made to."
Butler says so — but — hem. —

As now and then she caught his glance apace:
And how it was, she could not tell aright,
She loved to gaze upon his manly face,
Which tho' time had his ravages begun,
Appeared quite seemingly to look upon.

LVIII.

But soon their ogles and devotion ended;
  And, from the sacred structure, home they went;
Tho' neither to a *conquest* yet pretended.
  Still in their breasts some movings of consent
Appear'd — that if it e'er should be contended,
  That either side had won — each was content. . . .,
— A parley soon commenced — whether on the same day,
Or not, my present MSS. dont go to say.

LIX.

Whoe'er thought fit to watch the wily motions,
  Of two such amaratos, throughout the round
Of courtship, midnight revels with devotions,
  Need not be told, what harmony was found
Between them; — nor how full they were of notions —
  Or yet how love caresses did abound —
And those fond raptures and transporting blisses,
The young maid feels who dreams of "lover's kisses!"

LX.

The innocent reserve — the soft impression —
  The bashful "wavering look" — the "blush — enchanting" —
The "stolen glance" — the kind but coy expression,
  And trembling hand — and bosom lightly panting —
As forth was pour'd the *dearly* gain'd confession —
  And all love's ensignia were not found wanting: —
At least according to the letter of the story; —
At all events, ye have the case before ye.

LXI.

Rosalie pass'd full many a sleeping night, —
  Or if she slept — 'twas but to dream of bowers,
And shady groves, that charm the lover's sight,
  Baptiste, the wedding ring, and bridal flowers —
That soon her blushing beauties should bedight.
  While Baptiste chid the heavy rolling hours,
And his wild passions seem'd all noise and riot —
Because, poor soul he could not keep them — quiet.

LXII.

Hope, fear, distrust and killing jealousy,
  In high rebellion rose: — he'd felt the pain,

Of disappointment's bitter cruelty,
   Nor much could wish to be her sport again. . . .
At length the day arrives — new expectancy,
   Tiptoe, his better sense could scarce restrain: —
Indeed to make a *trope* of his disease, —
He felt like one *barefooted* on *hot peas*!

LXIII.

Baptiste had wealth, and did I think make o'er
   Of his abundance, by notarial deed,
Some two three thousand pounds, or more,
   To his attended spouse — lest time, indeed,
Should, unawares, come knocking at his door,
   And prove "the best friend, is a friend in need;"
'Twas a good plan — but over and above,
He wished to shew his strong impassioned — love!

LXIV.

"Precaution is a virtue" — we are told,
   I do believe it, as oft demonstrated,
And an acknowledged maxim from of old, —
   Among the luckless, prosperous or ill fated;
And *"maxims"* and *"old saws"* when they unfold,
   And leave the path, plainly delineated,
Which we should fellow, nothing on earth should hinder,
Our following them — so says Peter Pindar.

LXV.

And Peter knew — at least he should have known —
   But whether Peter knew, with all his knowledge,
The law of *marriage contracts* — it is not shown
   By his Biographer — He'd been thro' College,
But was no F. R. S. himself did own;
   Yet he might indeed have understood the tollage
Of London-Bridge; — nor let this shame us,
One may know many things, yet be an ignoramus

LXVI.

On others,* Peter further saith. "He lies."
   Who says it? Aye, but then he told the truth,
Of a great king, (and kings are always wise,)
   Who, famed for wisdom from his very youth,
Knew not the *"physiology of pies,"*
   Strange though it doth appear and most uncouth.
For when a "Dumpling" had been set before him,
He stared, as if a Samuel was to score him

---

* *An honest man may be a bitter bad logician." — SWIFT.*

LXVII.

In pieces, and — you know the tale no doubt —
    I shall suppose it — and again proceed.
Those who have wisdom (many are without,)
    Will own, I think, the justness of my creed,
Altho' it be not orthodox throughout,
    That a good marriage contract is indeed,
A wise precaution — since to prove I'm able,
Marriage a *"rente viagere et non rachetable,"*

LXVIII.

Of a man's patience, or at least, affections,
    Which are, *"par privilege, hypothequé."*
And of all bitter, sorry-faced reflections,
    That come across one, in life's wintry way —
None are more bitter than those cursed *"ejections,"*
    From an estate — when he has debts to pay,
And, has not, the "wherewith," to go and pay them, —
Nor faithful friend, with timely aid to stay them.

LXIX.

This by the way. — The lovely blooming bride
    Appeared in all her robes of hearty drest: —
Her gown was lace, figured and flounced, beside
    A plain plush zone encircleing her breast,
(I know not why) a burning crimson dyed: —
    A white lace frill, her flutt'ring bosom prest,
A cap of bobbin-nett — and to complete,
Shoes of the whitest silk bedeck'd her feet.

LXX.

I'd nigh forgot her downy gloves of kid,
    And sparkling clasp that held her crimson zone,
Whose beauty shone resplendant and unbid,
    Bright as the lustre of the diamond stone,
I would add more — but — modesty forbid —
    Unless the ring that on her finger shone —
But not her bridal ring — 'twas I suppose
A fond momento of her youthful beaux!

LXXI.

A fancy trinket. But may Heav'n forgive me,
    If in the course of life's short chequer'd day,
I give fair Lady (lest she might deceive me,)
    Aught then a tender heart; which if she play
Too rudely with, or slighted — (and believe me,
    That such may n'er occur I often pray,)
Could I retrieve it — and regain possession —
I'd not repent in hasted a like — transgression.

LXXII.

And this — I wish to have well understood —
I mean in love and courtship
        * * * * * * * * *
          * * * * * * * * *
        * * * * * * * * * *
          * * * * * * * *
        * * * * * * * * *
          * * * * * * * *

LXXIII.

The Bridegroom's dress — some small refinement shew'd,
   His coat was black, or of a sombre hue,
Best superfine — and cut quite à la mode, —
   Vest silk — and "inexpressibles" of blue,
With white cravat superbly double bowed —
   A wide plain frill, left full as plain to view —
Pinn'd with a Broach, in which was neatly set
A little portrait of his niece Josette.

LXXIV.

The *Angélus* had toll'd — all expectation —
   'Twas five — one hour — the fatal knot is tied —
Hubbub and noise succeed in preparation. . . .
   Her bosom throbb'd — flutter'd — she smil'd — then sigh'd,
While Baptiste look'd all joy and animation —
   So soon to have a "blushing, blooming Bride."
Meantime the half officious waiting throng,
   Chaunted in chorus some obstreperous song.

LXXV.

I think 'twas in the gloomy month October,
   When rugged Autumn with his winter shocks,
Made nature's face look quite downcast and sober,
   Like the lone desert, or rough mountain rocks,
Barren and verdureless; and did unrobe her,
   Of her fair garments, and light flowing locks, —
Indeed she look'd most mournfully baldheaded,
A situation of all others to be dreaded.

LXXVI.

I would not say she wore a wig — but then
   Such desolation did her looks pervade —
Such pensive stillness mid the wood and glen,
   Save when the piercing blast swept thro' the glade,
And echoed from the mountains back again, —
   While angry clouds their lengthen'd skirts display'd —
You'd thought — a bleak Canadian fall, or winter, —
The worst of times for — Poet or for — Printer.

LXXVII.

I do — whether *en campagne* or *en ville*,
　　They're very much like Byron's poetry —
Now here — now there — now sideways or uphill, —
　　Or in a *cahot*, if there's snow d'ye see, —
And if there's none — why have it if you will,
　　In mud or ditch, as best it pleases ye,
Both may be had, or either at your option,
As easy, as a son or daughter — *by adoption!*

LXXVIII.

Now off to Church: first in the clan appear,
　　The fair Bride and *fille d'honneur* in their coach;
Follow'd by Jacques, Etienne and Casimir; —
　　Each as related in the line approach —
While Jean Baptiste *"in tow"* brings up the rear,
　　With Bazile the groom's man, in a Barouche. —
Each blade with *Demoiselle* of "note and fame,"
Drove like old Jehu — off to *Notre Dame*.

LXXIX.

And let them go — for me, 'tis much too early,
　　To go to church — let us suppose it over —
That they are married — and return'd quite cheerly —
　　Transformed to "man and wife" from "sweet and lover."
　　　　* 　* 　* 　* 　* 　* 　* 　* 　*
　　　　　* 　* 　* 　* 　* 　* 　* 　*
　　　　* 　* 　* 　* 　* 　* 　* 　* 　*
　　　　　* 　* 　* 　* 　* 　* 　* 　*

LXXX.

Assembled *chez son père* we find *Antoine*,
　　The venerable father of our her;
And only sister the fair *Rosaline*,
　　Gallanted by *Toussaint* her cavilero.
His brothers *Hypolite*, *Ignace* and *Aqueline*,
　　Dandies of the "first water;" — Bombardero
The father with the mother of the bride,
And *Angelique*, a maiden aunt by mother's side.

LXXXI.

There was *Pierre* Catgut with his bow and rosin,
　　And *Docteur Crispin* whom the whole world knows, —
With nostrums and prescriptions by the dozen,
　　To kill or cure — no matter how it goes —
And there was * * * * *Avocat* and *cozen*,
　　With "whereas, whys, and wherefores, and ergoes;"
And lots of friends, relations, cousin german,
Than write whose names I'd sooner write a sermon.

LXXXII.

Oh 'twould have done one good to see the shaking
  Of hands, — the kissing — wishing them "much joy." —
No look downcast — nor bitter sad heart aching
  Unless from wounds of Venus — roving boy.
So like Newyears — or Christmas merry making,
  Where all is jollity without alloy,
That one could wish, without repentance dreading,
This life were all a Christmas or a wedding.

LXXXIII.

Vin rouge and *Teneriffe* — in great profusion,
  With *"votre santé madame,"* — *"Monsieur votre,"* —
Was drank, who bow'd *"merci,"* — in sweet delusion,
  Of being happier far, than *aucune autre*
Mortals on *Terra Firma* could be. Confusion
  Laughter and mirth, which so much abound *en notre*
Assemblées — now echoed throughout the train,
As if, half Bedlam was let loose again.

LXXXIV.

But one may drink of pleasure to the brim —
  And feast with mirth his wild imagination;
Pale hunger comes, with visage wan and grim,
  To chase far hence their heartless fascination: —
And tho' our souls in bright Elysium swim,
  Or seem at least, — we feel his incitation,
And leave our folly — to become a fool —
And tho' all else — we never eat by rule.

LXXXV.

Here marrying, mirth and kissing could not do —
  That guest who comes forever uninvited; —
And digs we're told, the hedge and stone wall thro',
  A longing passion in their breasts excited.
'Twas naught uncommon — yet 'twas something new —
  Hunger and thirst voraciously united —
And all, at length, old, young, from first to last,
Sat down, to a good, wholesome, kind repast.

LXXXVI.

Imprimis; first there was *Boeuf à la mode,*
  Stuff'd with good onions, garlicks, sage and thyme, —
A jambon ragoo'd, — what is nothing odd,
  Good warm pea soup — (a favourite dish of mine)
Blood pudding, *poudin de Ris,* beans in the pod —
  Spices, sweetmeats of ev'ry name and clime.
Their Liquors too were *"charmant"* and *"superbe,"*
Would that I had a glass my muse to curb,

LXXXVII.

Or animate; being not of the persuasion,
  Who deem a "social drop" a woeful sin,
(Well weighing the occurence and occasion,)
  After a wedding feast; — a glass of gin,
Or shrub, or whiskey, or — I hate evasion —
  Tho' some who good dame Muse's smiles would win,
Chose champagne, or madeira, — I would think most handy,
Were I to have my choice — a glass or two of brandy.

LXXXVIII.

A glass or two — I mean just *quantum suff*;
  Tho', as to that, I would not be particular;
It stands to reason that "enough's enough,"
  Since with too much, one cant keep perpendicular —
And surfeiting I hate. — I hate a gruff,
  Old toper, — and especially vernacular —
Or otherwise — and finally — of late —
Some things I used to love, I almost hate:

LXXXIX.

And *vice versa*, — but loving or hating,
  Or this, or that, I must forsooth proceed,
Matters like these, are scarcely worth debating, —
  When old Pegassus canters at full speed,
And the good reader is impatient waiting,
  The *"finish"* — Id nigh forgot it — sad indeed —
The feasting o'er — what follow'd is — uncertain;
For want of facts I'm forc'd to drop the — *curtain!*

LXXXX.

"La Farce est faite" — my hero disappears —
  Alas! 'tis thus with all things — transitory;
Carousals, revels, sorrow, grief and tears,
  The disappointments of an "old age hoary,"
When, with regret, we view our by-past years,
  Must have an end, — as here must end my — story!
And since it is so — reader be assur'd,
"A CURELESS MALADY MUST BE ENDUR'D."

THE END